Before They Were Famous

Amelia Earhart

Written by Stephen Krensky
Illustrated by Bobbie Houser

A Crabtree Crown Book

CRABTREE
Publishing Company
www.crabtreebooks.com

School-to-Home Support for Caregivers and Teachers

This appealing book is designed to teach students about core subject areas. Students will build upon what they already know about the subject, and engage in topics that they want to learn more about. Here are a few guiding questions to help readers build their comprehension skills. Possible answers appear here in red.

Before Reading:

What do I know about this topic?

- *I know that Amelia Earhart was a famous airplane pilot.*
- *I know that her airplane went down over the ocean, and they never found the airplane.*

What do I want to learn about this topic?

- *I want to learn why experts couldn't find the plane when it was first missing.*
- *I want to learn more about her life when she was growing up.*

During Reading:

I'm curious to know...

- *I'm curious to know what event in Amelia's life made her want to fly.*
- *I'm curious to know how old Amelia was when she saw an airplane for the first time.*

How is this like something I already know?

- *I knew there had to be an event or a person who sparked Amelia's interest in flying.*
- *I knew that Amelia was one of the most famous female pilots in the United States.*

After Reading:

What was the author trying to teach me?

- *I think that the author wanted to teach me that it often takes hard work and dedication to achieve our goals.*
- *I think the author wanted to teach me that Amelia saved her money so she could take flying lessons.*

How did the photographs and captions help me understand more?

- *The photographs helped me to understand more about her family and where she came from.*
- *The captions taught me additional facts about the time period that Amelia lived in.*

Table of Contents

Nursing Ambitions

Amelia Earhart was busy.

Actually, she was busier than she had ever been in her life. It was the winter of 1918, and 20-year-old Amelia was a nurse's aide in Toronto, Canada. Hundreds of wounded Canadian soldiers had been injured in the Great War in Europe. Now they had returned home, but they were hardly cured.

Fun Facts

The Great War, later known as World War I, lasted from 1914-1918.

Amelia's duties included whatever would help. She cleaned wounds, gave out medicine, washed floors, and helped prepare meals.

Fun Facts

Amelia took a Voluntary Aid course and a Red Cross first-aid class before becoming a nurse's aide.

Among the soldiers were a number of pilots, and Amelia loved hearing their stories about flying high in the sky.

Amelia had never expected to end up nursing in Toronto. But there she was. Born in Kansas, she had lived in several places, from Iowa to Minnesota.

Fun Facts

Amelia's family moved a lot because her father kept changing jobs.

She wrote poems that had never been published. She could dance and swim and play basketball. But nothing seemed to excite her or fuel her dreams for the future.

Ups and Downs

In some ways, the most exciting thing that had ever happened to Amelia was building a little roller coaster when she was seven years old. Her uncle had helped, and the ramp reached up 8 feet (2 meters) off the ground.

1908 Iowa State Fair

Fun Facts

Amelia saw her first airplane at the Iowa State Fair in 1908.

On her first ride, her wooden cart jumped off the rails and sailed through the air before crashing to the ground. The cart was smashed to pieces, but Amelia survived with only a swollen lip.

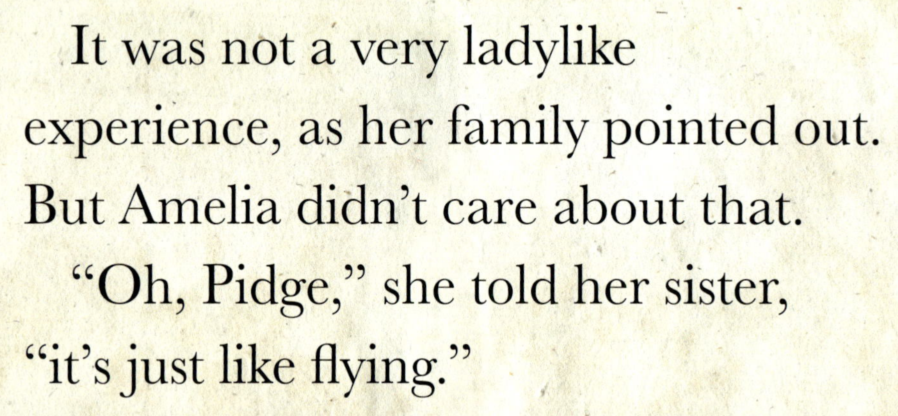

It was not a very ladylike experience, as her family pointed out. But Amelia didn't care about that.

"Oh, Pidge," she told her sister, "it's just like flying."

SISTERS

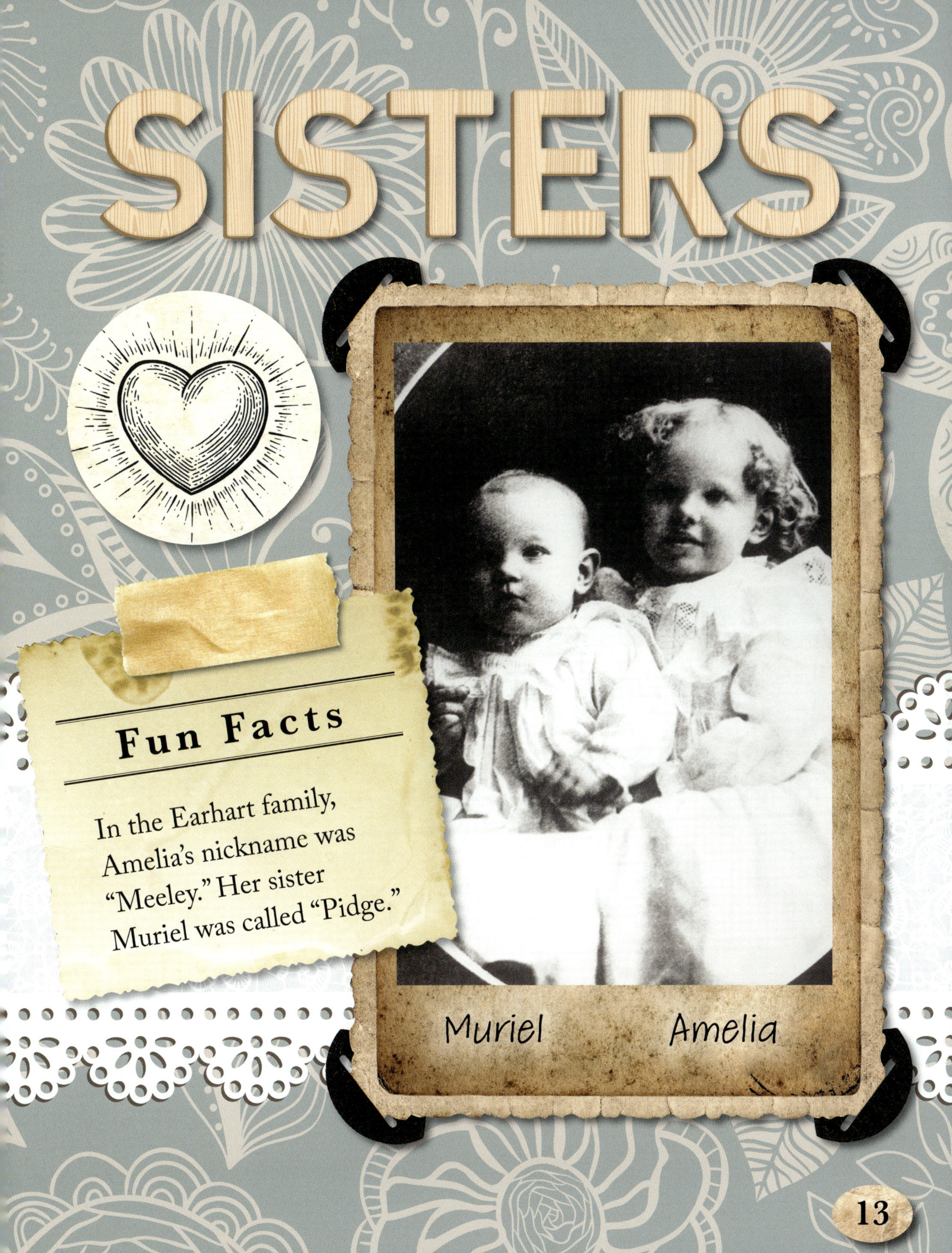

Fun Facts

In the Earhart family, Amelia's nickname was "Meeley." Her sister Muriel was called "Pidge."

Head in the Clouds

As a nurse's aide, Amelia worked from seven in the morning till seven at night. But she still had some time off, and one day she and a friend went to an air show.

The pilots were showing off, doing spins and **barrel rolls**. One of the pilots spotted the two young women watching from a clearing, and he decided to dive right at them.

Amelia might have run or ducked or at least screamed. Certainly, the pilot probably thought that she would.

Instead, she never moved. The roar of the plane, the whoosh of the air around it, was thrilling to her.

"I did not understand it at the time," she wrote later, "but I believe that little red airplane said something to me as it swished by."

Fun Facts

The fastest airplanes in 1918 could go about 100 miles (160 kilometers) an hour.

After the war ended, Amelia returned to the United States. At first she began studying to become a doctor, but then decided she didn't want to work with patients. She thought maybe medical research would suit her better.

Fun Facts

Amelia's first flight cost $10—equal to about $165 today.

However, on a trip to California to visit her parents, she went to an air show and had her first ride in an airplane. "By the time I had got two or three hundred feet off the ground," she said, "I knew I had to fly."

But becoming a pilot was expensive. Amelia could not afford the flying lessons. So she worked part-time as a truck driver, a photographer, and a secretary at the local telephone company to save as much money as possible.

Fun Facts

The average hourly wage in 1920 was about 33 cents an hour.

Taking Off

Amelia finally had her first lesson on January 3, 1921. In order to get to the airfield, she had to take a bus to the end of the line and then walk 3 miles (4.8 km) to get to the airfield.

But she didn't complain. If she could learn to fly, it was worth it.

Fun Facts

Amelia took flying lessons for several months before she was **qualified** to fly solo.

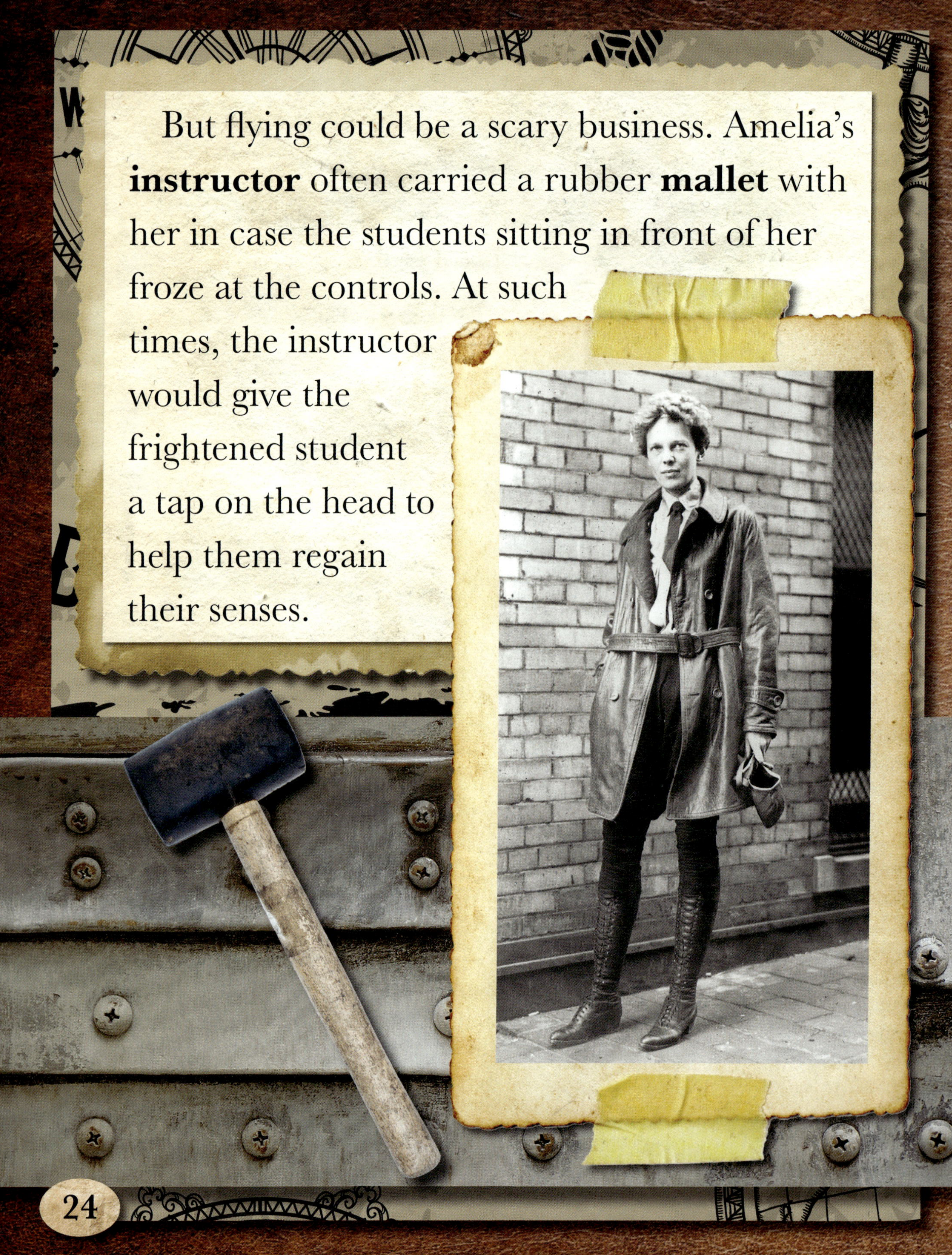

But flying could be a scary business. Amelia's **instructor** often carried a rubber **mallet** with her in case the students sitting in front of her froze at the controls. At such times, the instructor would give the frightened student a tap on the head to help them regain their senses.

Amelia embraced everything about being a pilot. She bought **breeches**, goggles, and a leather jacket, the kind of clothing pilots wore. She also gradually cut her hair quite short.

Fun Facts

Amelia slept in her leather jacket for several nights so it wouldn't look so new.

As Amelia gained more flying time, she realized that pilots were not just showing off when they practiced spinning and rolling and engine **stalls** at air shows. If their engines or other equipment failed during a flight, a spin or a stall might come next. If they had practiced what to do in that situation, they wouldn't **panic**. And not panicking could save lives.

Neta with Amelia

Anita Snook, 1980

Fun Facts

Amelia's teacher was Anita Snook, known as Neta, one of the first female pilots in the United States.

Aiming Higher and Higher

Amelia took another piloting step forward when she bought her first plane, a yellow Kinner Airster she nicknamed "the Canary."

And on October 22, 1922, when she flew the Canary to an **altitude** of 14,000 feet (4,267 meters), Amelia set a new world record for female pilots. At that point she entered the record books for the first time. Her career was really taking off.

"The Canary"

Fun Facts

On May 15, 1923, Earhart became the 16th woman in the United States to be issued an international pilot's license.

Amelia Earhart was born in Kansas six years before the Wright Brothers made their first flight in 1903. As a young female pilot in the1920s, she set several **aviation** *records. Notably, she was the first woman to cross the Atlantic Ocean in an airplane, doing so as a passenger in 1928. Four years later, she piloted a plane solo across the Atlantic.*

In 1937, Amelia Earhart and her **navigator** *Fred Noonan vanished somewhere in the South Pacific Ocean on a flight planned to take them around the world. Their final resting place remains a mystery.*

GLOSSARY

altitude
The height of an object compared to the ground or sea level

aviation
The flying of an aircraft

barrel roll
A movement by an airplane in which it rolls all the way over in a circle before taking up its original position

breeches
A kind of short pants that are fastened just below the knee

instructor
A teacher specializing in a particular subject area

mallet
A kind of hammer with a wide rubber head

navigator
A person who directs a route for travel

panic
A sudden feeling of being upset or fearful

qualified
Officially trained to do a certain job or activity

stalls
A condition when an airplane is angled sharply upward and loses lift under the wings

INDEX

COMPREHENSION QUESTIONS

Where did Amelia serve as a nurse's aide?

In what month did Amelia have her first flying lesson?

How high did Amelia fly her airplane to set a record for female pilots?

ABOUT THE AUTHOR

Stephen Krensky is the award-winning author of more than 150 fiction and nonfiction books for children. He and his wife Joan live in Lexington, Massachusetts, and he happily spends as much time as possible with his grown children and not-so-grown grandchildren.

Written by: Stephen Krensky
Illustrations by: Bobbie Houser
Art direction and layout by: Bobbie Houser
Series Development: James Earley
Proofreader: Petrice Custance
Educational Consultant: Marie Lemke M.Ed.
Print Coordinator: Katherine Berti

Photographs: t = Top, c = Center, b = Bottom, l = Left, r = Right
Alamy: Ken Hackett: p. 8 c; Pictorial Press Ltd: p. 23 c; Scherl/Süddeutsche Zeitung Photo: p. 24 r; Aviation History Collection: p. 27 c; Science History Images: p. 28; Getty: Bettmann: p. 13 r; Granger: pp. 4, 8 t; LOC: p. 25 r; NASA: p. 27 b; Shutterstock: Vectorcarrot: cover tl, pp. 7, 23 tl; Everett Collection: cover bl, p. 29 b; Graeme Dawes: cover br, p. 25 tc; PHILIPIMAGE: p. 5 tl; Keith Tarrier: p. 5 tr; Everett Collection: p. 5 cl; Klaus Nicodem: p. 5 cr; Ljupco Smokovski: p. 5 bl; Bankrx: p. 6 tl; lynea: p. 6 tr; chippix: p. 6 bl; Glevalex: p. 6 br; Alexander Varbenov: p. 8 b; Roberto Castillo: p. 10 t; Alexandr Shevchenko: p. 10 b; Ollie The Designer: p. 13 t; Very_Very: p. 13 l; VectorPot: pp. 14, 17 bl; Petr Bonek: pp. 15 t, 17 t; Peter Baxter: p. 15 c; AVA Bitter: p. 15 b; Ensuper: p. 17 br; ducu59us: p. 18 tl; Uncle Leo: pp. 18 tc, 21 b; David Franklin: p. 18 tr; dalmingo: p. 18 b; Lou Oates: p. 20; MoreVector: p. 21 tl; RetroClipArt: p. 21 tr; BrAt82: p. 21 c; Kudryashka: p. 23 b; Phatanin Tantikarun: p. 24 l; Elala: p. 25 l; AkimD: p. 27 t; AKaiser: p. 29 t

Library and Archives Canada Cataloguing in Publication

Available at the Library and Archives Canada

Library of Congress Cataloging-in-Publication Data

Available at the Library of Congress

Crabtree Publishing Company

www.crabtreebooks.com 1-800-387-7650

In Canada: We acknowledge the financial support of the Government of Canada through the Canada Book Fund for our publishing activities.

Published in the United States
Crabtree Publishing
347 Fifth Avenue
Suite 1402-145
New York, NY, 10016

Published in Canada
Crabtree Publishing
616 Welland Ave.
St. Catharines, ON
L2M 5V6

Printed in the U.S.A./072022/CG20220201